Life Cycles

Butterfly

Louise Spilsbury

Raintree

www.raintreepublishers.co.uk

Visit our website to find out more information about **Raintree** books.

To order:

☎ Phone 44 (0) 1865 888112

▤ Send a fax to 44 (0) 1865 314091

▢ Visit the Raintree Bookshop at **raintreepublishers.co.uk** to browse our catalogue and order online.

First published in Great Britain by Raintree, Halley Court, Jordan Hill, Oxford OX2 8EJ, part of Harcourt Education.
Raintree is a registered trademark of Harcourt Education Ltd.

Editorial: Charlotte Guillain and Diyan Leake
Design: Michelle Lisseter
Picture Research: Maria Joannou and Debra Weatherley
Production: Lorraine Hicks

Originated by Dot Gradations
Printed and bound in China by South China Printing Company

ISBN 1 844 21251 3 (hardback)
07 06 05 04 03
10 9 8 7 6 5 4 3 2 1

ISBN 1 844 21256 4 (paperback)
08 07 06 05
10 9 8 7 6 5 4 3 2

British Library Cataloguing in Publication Data
Spilsbury, Louise
Butterfly
571.8'1578
A full catalogue record for this book is available from the British Library.

Acknowledgements
The publishers would like to thank the following for permission to reproduce photographs: Alamy Images p. 21; Ardea (Steve Hopkin) pp. 4, 8, 23 (female); Bruce Coleman (Kim Taylor) pp. 5, 19; Nature Photographers (Geoff Du Feu) pp. 16, 17, 23 (nectar, proboscis); Nature Picture Library (Hans Christoph Kapel) pp. 9, 12, 13, 14, 23 (chrysalis, jaws); Oxford Scientific Films pp. 10 (Raymond Blythe), 11 (John Woolmer), 22 (Robert Parks); Papilio pp. 6 (Robert Pickett), 7 (Robert Pickett), 15 (Robert Pickett), 18 (Laura Sivell), 23 (hatch, Robert Pickett; nectar, Laura Sivell); Science Photo Library (Gregory Dimijian) p. 20

Cover photograph of a butterfly, reproduced with permission of NHPA (Robert Tompson)

Every effort has been made to contact copyright holders of any material reproduced in this book. Any omissions will be rectified in subsequent printings if notice is given to the publishers.

Contents

Some words are shown in bold, **like this**. They are explained in the glossary on page 23.

What is a butterfly?

This is a butterfly.

Butterflies are **insects** with colourful wings.

Butterflies start life inside tiny eggs.

This picture makes the eggs
look big.

Where do butterflies lay eggs?

A **female** butterfly lays her eggs on plants.

Then she flies away.

After some time, caterpillars **hatch** out of the eggs.

What do caterpillars eat?

Caterpillars eat leaves.

They crawl slowly over plants to find food.

jaws

Caterpillars bite off pieces of leaf with their **jaws**.

How do caterpillars grow?

Caterpillars eat until they are too big for their skin.

Then their old skin splits and comes off.

There is a new skin underneath.

Caterpillars change their skin four or five times as they grow.

How do caterpillars become butterflies?

When a caterpillar is fully grown, it is ready to become a butterfly.

First it hangs upside-down in a quiet place.

Then the last caterpillar skin comes off.

Beneath it is the **chrysalis**.

What is a chrysalis?

The **chrysalis** is a hard case that keeps the caterpillar safe.

The caterpillar changes into a butterfly inside the chrysalis.

This butterfly is nearly ready to come out of its chrysalis.

When do butterflies leave the chrysalis?

When a butterfly is fully grown, the **chrysalis** splits open.

The butterfly wriggles out.

At first the butterfly's wings
are wet.

When they are dry the butterfly
can fly.

What do butterflies eat?

Butterflies drink a sugary juice called **nectar**.

They find nectar in flowers.

Butterflies suck up nectar with a hollow tongue called a **proboscis**.

This rolls up when they finish drinking.

How do butterflies keep safe?

This butterfly is the same colour as the leaves.

This helps it hide from animals that try to eat butterflies.

Butterflies fly to escape danger and to find food.

They also fly to find somewhere to lay eggs of their own.

Butterfly map

head

wing

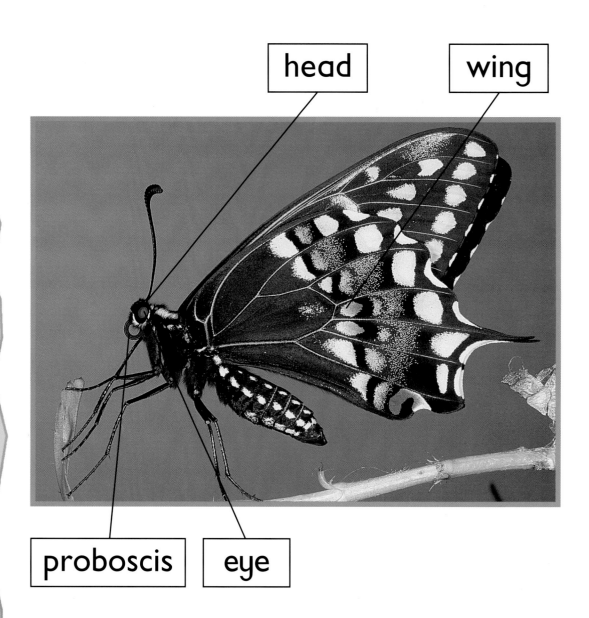

proboscis

eye

Glossary

 **chrysalis** hard case in which a caterpillar changes into a butterfly

 **female** female animals can have babies or lay eggs that hatch into babies

 **hatch** come out of an egg

 **insects** animals that have six legs and usually two pairs of wings

 **jaws** hard mouthparts that can bite

 **nectar** sweet juice in the centre of a flower

 **proboscis** long tube that some insects use like a straw to drink with

Index